DEBRIS

TIDBITS TO BIG-BATCH COOKING

BETH PARROTT

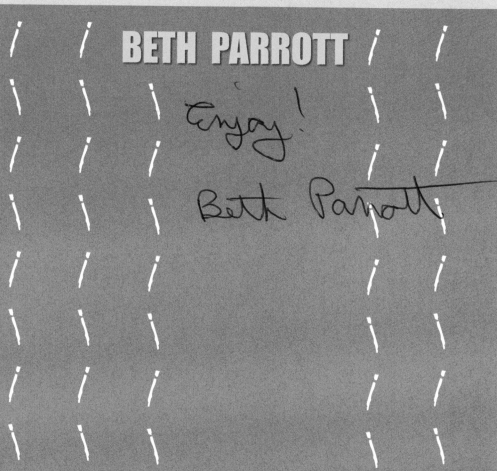

Enjoy!

Beth Parrott

Printed in the United States of America

Editor: Holly Iglesias
Front and Back Cover Images: Pat McDonald Fowler
Hot Sauce Image, page 29: Earl Simmons
Photography: Bren Dendy – www.brenphotography.net
Book Design: Ginger Graziano – www.gingergraziano.com

To my friends and family
who have gathered in my kitchen

TABLE OF CONTENTS

INTRODUCTION

I have been fortunate in my lifetime to live and travel in beautiful places with rich culinary heritages—South Georgia, Iran, Key West, New Orleans and different regions of Mexico. Georgia is about fried chicken, okra, gravy, and biscuits. Iran exposed me to basmati rice, yogurt, pomegranates, and bazaars full of fragrant spices. Key West is the Cuban influence—black beans, picadillo, café con leche. New Orleans is a combination of French, Spanish, and Cajun flavors—crawfish étouffée, Andouille sausage, gumbo. Mexican cooking is some of the most flavorful and most beautiful in my experience—carrot soup, colorful salsas, Oaxacan moles.

Each of these cuisines shares similar qualities—fresh, simple and colorful. Each of these cultures is known for its love of gathering friends and families to share a fragrant, bountiful meal.

My cooking, my recipes and my desire to gather and feed family and friends are simply a distillation of these regions, cultures, and cuisines. Gathering for a Mardi Gras parade. Providing a dish to a family with a new baby. Making soup for a friend recovering from surgery. My response to major life events—drama, trauma, birth, death, and everything in between—is to cook a large batch of something nurturing and to gather people to enjoy it.

MY COOKING PHILOSOPHY

I love to cook—sometimes. Some days are meant for cooking; others are not.

My basic food philosophy is that if you have to eat, it should be delicious. It doesn't need to be gourmet, just tasty. Food should be healthy—organic when reasonable, fresh ingredients, lean, something green everyday.

To honor the idea that you can't cook every day and that food should be reasonably healthy, tasty and economical, I have developed a style of cooking that allows for large batches of food that can be frozen for later consumption.

When my boys were born in the early 90's, our life was overwhelmingly busy—two fulltime jobs, two boys two years apart. We could not afford to eat out often from an economic as well as a caloric perspective. Consequently, I would take a day off of work and cook a big pot of beans, a big pot of soup and a pot of Debris. We would have three meals prepared for immediate consumption. The bonus would be filling the freezer with instant meals. Before serving my people, I would "pay myself first" by putting two containers of each dish in the freezer.

Over the years, I have developed several recipes that freeze well and can be mixed and matched. You can create many meals simply by thawing out the dish, cooking some pasta or rice and serving with a fresh salad.

These are great recipes for feeding large groups of people. I have been known to have spontaneous parties with the contents of my freezer. When we travel, it is always wonderful to return home knowing there is something delicious and healthy to pull out of the freezer after days or weeks of eating road food.

This type of cooking requires an investment in time to make the basic dishes—the Debris, the roasted tomatoes, the beans. But, the dividends arrive when it's time to serve a meal from the freezer, which is a matter of quick assembly.

This type of cooking is not only convenient; it should also be fun. All the recipes are simple, forgiving and open for your interpretation. Each one can be modified according to your available time. For example, use a jar of your favorite salsa instead of making a fresh salsa, or use frozen vegetables instead of fresh. If you have a favorite meatball or meatloaf recipe, use it.

The last chapter, "Lagniappe," contains recipes for quick and easy foods that don't fit into a specific category, such as the Cabbage and Red Bean Cole Slaw, which is great for potlucks, or the Southwestern Chicken Casserole, which feeds many people quickly and inexpensively.

NOTE: Many of these recipes can be modified for gluten-free diets as well as vegetarian diets.

BUILDING BLOCKS

There are a few things that make this type of cooking easy—same size containers, a well-stocked pantry and a few basic recipes.

In order to maximize freezer space, it is helpful to have the same size of freezer containers. I use one-quart size round containers for soups and beans, and two-cup containers for Debris and tomato sauce. Choose the size container that accommodates your family needs. Be sure to label each container. It's worth the time.

In addition to basics in the freezer, it is helpful to have a pantry stocked with items that can be used to assemble meals easily.

PANTRY BASICS:

Cans of chopped tomatoes
Cans of red beans, white beans, black beans, and refried beans
Cans of corn
Cans of green chilies
Cans of organic chicken stock (low salt) and vegetable stock
Jars of tomato sauce like Bertolli with olive oil, basil, and garlic
Jars of red and green salsas
Pasta
Orzo
Rice
Tortilla chips
Instant mashed potatoes
Cornbread mix
Taco shells

Most of the recipes in the book call for some very basic components like rice, salsa or stock. This section includes recipes for these basics.

CHEESE GRITS

(serves 4)

1 C white or yellow grits
4 C water
1 tsp. salt
½ tsp. pepper
2 tbsp. butter
1 C grated cheese—cheddar and Monterey Jack

Bring water and salt to a boil.

Add grits and reduce heat to low. Cover

Cook for 20 minutes, stirring occasionally to keep the grits from sticking to the pot.

Add pepper, butter, and cheese.

Stir.

The grits should be thick, not soupy.

CHICKEN OR VEGETABLE STOCK

Bones of 2 roasted chickens
2 onions, quartered
3 carrots
3 stalks celery
1 head garlic, cut in half
1 tbsp. each of thyme, basil, oregano, and salt
10 peppercorns
4 qt. water

Place all the ingredients in a large stockpot, uncovered.

Simmer until the liquid is reduced by half—about 4 hours.

Stir occasionally.

Strain the stock through a colander.

Strain a second time through a wire mesh colander.

TIDBITS

Use in the dish you are making and freeze the remainder for later use.

If you want to make a vegetable stock, leave out the chicken.

If time is an issue, use prepared stock from the grocery store.

CORN CAKE

(serves 8)

1-½ C flour
½ C cornmeal
¼ C sugar
1 tbsp. baking powder
½ tsp. salt
1 C milk
⅓ C melted butter
2 eggs, beaten
1 15-oz. can corn, drained

Preheat oven to 400 degrees.

Combine the dry ingredients.

Add the milk, butter, eggs, and corn.

Mix well.

Pour into a greased 9 x 9" square pan.

Bake for 30 minutes or until golden brown and firm.

Add a small can of chopped green chilies for extra flavor.

If time is an issue, use a cornbread mix or buy cornbread from the grocery store bakery.

MASHED POTATOES

(serves 8)

3 lb. potatoes cut into quarters (no need to peel)
8 C water
1 to 2 C milk
4 tbsp. butter
1 tsp. salt
½ tsp. pepper

In a 2-quart saucepan, boil the water and add the potatoes.

Reduce to a simmer. Cover.

Cook for 30 minutes, or until the potatoes are tender.

Drain the potatoes and return to the saucepan.

Add the milk, butter, salt, and pepper.

Mash the ingredients together until smooth and creamy.

If time is an issue, use
instant mashed potatoes
following the directions on
the package.

POACHED EGGS

(serves 4)

8 eggs
Water

Heat the water to boil in a 2" deep skillet with a lid.

Reduce the heat to simmer.

Crack each egg and gently add to the water.

Once all the eggs have been added, cover and simmer for 3 minutes for medium eggs, 5 minutes for harder eggs.

Remove each egg from the pan with a slotted spoon.

RICE

(4 servings)

1 C rice
2 C water
1 tsp. olive oil
½ tsp. salt

In a 2-quart saucepan, put the water, olive oil, and salt.

Bring to a boil.

Add rice and cover the pot.

Reduce to a simmer for 20 minutes or until the water has evaporated.

TIDBITS

Different types of rice have different cooking times. For example, brown rice takes longer.

Read the package directions for the specific rice.

Experiment with different types of rice like Basmati rice or Jasmine rice.

I use a rice cooker, using the same 1:2 ratio of rice to water.

SALSA

(serves 8)

2 C fresh tomatoes, finely chopped
1 C green onions, finely chopped
1 C red bell pepper, finely chopped
4 cloves garlic, finely chopped
2 jalapeño peppers, seeded and finely chopped
½ C cilantro, finely chopped
Juice of 2 limes
1 tsp. salt
1 tsp. chili powder
1 tbsp. olive oil

Combine all ingredients in a bowl.

Mix well.

Refrigerate until ready to use.

Add a can of corn and a can of black beans to a basic salsa recipe.

Try adding a diced mango for a different twist.

DEBRIS

Debris is a delicious, versatile dish that might be reminiscent of the pot roast of your childhood but ramped up with New Orleans influence. My Debris recipe is a version of a dish served at Mother's, a sandwich shop in New Orleans. Mother's serves all types of meats—ham, turkey, and roast beef—that are freshly carved each day. All the bits and pieces that fall through the rack, too small to grace the famous sandwich, are combined with juices to create Debris.

Traditionally, it is served over grits or ladled on a Po'boy, which is New Orleans' version of a sandwich and always made with French bread. It is a great dish to feed a large group of people that will be eating at different times like during a Super Bowl party.

My rendition of Debris is not only a family favorite but out of town guests will call ahead to ensure that Debris will be on the menu during their visit. It can be served for dinner and usually people would like some left over to have for breakfast with poached eggs on top.

Just remember to "pay yourself first" because this stuff disappears.

BASIC DEBRIS

2 tbsp. olive oil
1 3 to 4 lb. sirloin tip roast or chuck roast
1 5 to 6 lb. pork butt, excess fat removed
2 large white onions, roughly chopped
3 large carrots, thinly sliced
1 10-oz. can Rotel tomatoes with green chilies
1 15-oz. can of diced tomatoes
6 cloves of garlic, roughly chopped
2 C red wine or beer
1 tbsp. each thyme, basil, oregano, Tabasco sauce
1 tbsp. salt
1 tsp. pepper
Water as needed

Preheat oven to 325 degrees.

In a large Dutch oven, heat the olive oil.

Brown the pork butt on all sides and remove from the Dutch oven.

Brown the beef on all sides.

Return the pork butt to the pot.

Add onion, carrots, tomatoes, garlic, and wine.

Add thyme, oregano, basil, salt, pepper, and Tabasco sauce.

Add enough water to cover the meat.

Cover the pot and bake for four hours.

After the first hour, turn the meat and stir.

Check the pot every hour, stirring the contents and shredding the meat as it begins to fall apart.

Add water as need to keep the ingredients moist.

The dish is done when the pork and the beef have completely fallen apart. The 4-hour cooking time is an average.

When the Debris is done, remove the bone from the pork butt and any extra fat.

DEBRIS AND GRITS
(serves 4)

4 C Basic Debris
4 C Cheese Grits (see Building Blocks)

Prepare Cheese Grits.

Heat Basic Debris.

Place 1C of Cheese Grits in a bowl and ladle 1 C of Basic Debris over it. Be sure to include some of the gravy.

Serve with a green salad and crusty French bread.

TIDBITS

This dish makes an excellent brunch when served with 2 poached eggs on top.

Serve it with any type of salsa for something different.

If you don't care for grits, serve the Debris over rice, biscuits, or cornbread.

DEBRIS PIE

(serves 4)

4 C Basic Debris, heated
4 C Mashed Potatoes (see Building Blocks)
16 oz. corn, frozen or canned, drained

Preheat oven to 350 degrees.

Grease a 9 x 9" casserole dish.

Cover the bottom with 2-3" of Debris.

Cover Debris with mashed potatoes, spreading evenly.

Sprinkle corn over mashed potatoes.

Cover with foil and bake for 45 minutes.

Remove foil and bake uncovered for 15 minutes.

Serve with a salad.

TIDBITS

The beauty of this dish is that it can be made ahead of time.

Best to bring to room temperature prior to heating.

Cheese of any sort can be added to the potatoes.

Make two 9 x 9" pans—one for dinner and one to freeze, i.e. pay yourself.

DEBRIS PO'BOYS (SANDWICHES)
(serves 4)

4 C Basic Debris, heated
1 loaf French bread or Ciabatta
½ C mayonnaise
½ C coarse ground mustard
8 slices Swiss cheese
1 C thinly sliced white cabbage
8 Kosher dill pickles, sliced lengthwise
Tabasco sauce

Blend mayonnaise and mustard together.

Slice the bread lengthwise and cut into 6-inch pieces.
Toast the bread lightly.

Make an assembly line with the ingredients:
Bread
Mayo/mustard sauce
Debris
Cheese
Cabbage
Pickles
Tabasco sauce

Po'boys are very
messy. Have lots of
napkins on hand.

Allow your guests to
assemble the sand-
wiches for themselves.

Spread sauce on both sides of bread
with a spatula.

Put ½ C Debris on one side of the
bread, 2 slices of cheese on the other.

Cover Debris with sliced cabbage.

Add 2 pickles and hot sauce to taste.

Combine the two halves.

DEBRIS TACOS

(serves 4)

4 C Basic Debris, heated
8 corn or flour tortillas
1 C grated queso fresco or cheese of your choice
1 C salsa—homemade (see Building Blocks) or jarred
½ C each finely chopped green onions, jalapeños peppers, and avocado
2 limes, quartered

Lightly brown tortillas on each side in a dry skillet. Cover them in a basket to keep warm.

Put bowls of cheese, salsa, condiments, and lime in the center of the table.

Place 2 tortillas on each plate and top with ¼ C Debris.

Allow everyone to add the remaining ingredients to their taste.

Encourage the use of a squeeze of lime as the last addition.

 TIDBITS

Use tostados in place of tortillas.

Try a green salsa.

Put refried black beans on the tortillas before adding the Debris.

Put all the ingredients over a bed of tortilla chips; add a can of black beans and corn to make nachos.

3

ROASTED TOMATOES

My house never smells better than when I'm roasting a batch of tomatoes with onions, garlic, and herbs.

At the height of tomato season, I roast a case of tomatoes from the farmers market at a time. I will do three or four cases over the summer to ensure having enough to get through the winter. There is nothing like pulling a container of roasted tomatoes out of the freezer on a cold winter night and serving it with meatballs and freshly grated Parmesan cheese.

The roasted tomatoes make an excellent pizza sauce or bruschetta sauce. Use these roasted tomatoes in a soup.

Once you make this recipe, you will realize it is well worth the effort.

BASIC ROASTED TOMATO SAUCE

NOTE: Use a 9 x 13" roasting pan with sides at least 2" high.

Large tomatoes, washed and cut into 6 to 8 wedges
Onions, peeled and roughly chopped—2 per pan
Garlic cloves, peeled—6 per pan
Olive oil—¼ C per pan
Dried thyme, oregano, basil—1 tbsp. each per pan
Salt and pepper—1 tsp. each per pan

Preheat oven to 275 degrees.

Place the herbs in the bottom of the pan.

Add the remaining ingredients and mix well.

Bake approximately 6 hours, stirring every hour.

Mixture will be very soupy for the first 2 to 3 hours.

As liquid evaporates, ingredients begin to caramelize, turning deep red.

When the liquid has evaporated 90%, remove dish from oven and cool.

TIDBITS

Each 9 x 13" pan yields 2 cups of sauce.

Most ovens can accommodate at least 3 roasting pans.

Freeze the sauce in 1- or 2-cup containers. The sauce is so thick and concentrated that a little bit goes a long way.

I like the sauce chunky, but you can run it through a food processor if you prefer a smooth sauce.

ROASTED TOMATO SAUCE WITH PASTA

(serves 4)

1 C Roasted Tomato Sauce
1 24-oz. jar tomato sauce
(I use Bertolli's with olive oil, basil, and garlic)
1 C dry red wine, such as Chianti
10 fresh basil leaves, chopped, or
  1 tsp. dried basil
½ tsp. red pepper flakes
Salt to taste
1 8-oz. package of egg fettuccine
1 C freshly grated Parmesan
cheese

Combine Roasted Tomato Sauce, jarred tomato sauce, wine, basil, and pepper flakes.

Simmer for 1 hour, stirring occasionally.

Prepare pasta according to directions.

To serve, place ½ C pasta in a bowl. Ladle 1 C of tomato sauce over the pasta. Sprinkle generously with grated cheese.

Quick, simple, and tastes of summer.

A green salad and fresh, crusty bread complete this meal.

TIDBITS

Slice a pound of mushrooms and sauté in 2 tbsp. of olive oil. Add to the tomato sauce for a vegetarian dish.

Brown 1 lb. of Italian sausage, drain the fat and add to the sauce. The sausage can remain in whole links, sliced into bite size pieces, or removed from the casing.

Better yet, add both mushrooms and sausage.

Place a grilled chicken breast over the sauce for a different dish.

One of my favorites is to buy Chicken Parmesan from the deli counter, heat it up, slice it and serve on top of the tomato sauce.

Add a container of Debris to the tomato sauce for a hearty meal.

ROASTED TOMATO SAUCE WITH MEATBALLS

(serves 4)

1 cup Roasted Tomato Sauce
1 24-oz. jar tomato sauce (I use Bertolli's with olive oil, basil, and garlic)
1 C dry red wine, such as Chianti
10 fresh basil leaves, chopped, or 1 tsp. dried basil
½ tsp. red pepper flakes
Salt to taste
1 8-oz. package egg fettuccine
2 lb. ground beef
1 lb. ground pork or Italian sausage
2 eggs
1 C breadcrumbs
1 tsp. salt
¼ tsp. cayenne pepper
1 tsp. oregano
8 cloves garlic, peeled, cut in half lengthwise
1 C freshly grated Parmesan cheese

Combine Roasted Tomato Sauce, jarred tomato sauce, wine, basil, and pepper flakes in a saucepan.

Simmer for 1 hour, stirring occasionally.

TIDBITS

The meatball recipe yields 16 meatballs.

Leftover meatballs can be frozen in sauce for later use or used in the following recipe for a meatball Po'boy sandwich.

If you don't have time to make meatballs, purchase uncooked meatballs at the deli counter.

Preheat the oven to 350 degrees.

While sauce is simmering, mix beef, sausage, eggs, breadcrumbs, salt, cayenne pepper, and oregano in a bowl.

Use ½ C of the mixture to form each meatball with your hands.

Place in a 9 x 13" baking dish.

Insert garlic clove half in top of each meatball.

Bake for 30 minutes.

Cook pasta according to package directions.

To serve, place ½ cup of pasta in a bowl with ½ cup of sauce and a meatball on top. Garnish with Parmesan cheese.

MEATBALL PO'BOYS (SANDWICHES)

(serves 4)

1 C leftover Roasted Tomato Sauce (from previous recipe)
4 meatballs
1 C grated mozzarella cheese
1 loaf of French bread

Heat the tomato sauce and meatballs.

Slice the French bread lengthwise and into 6" sections.

Lightly toast the cut side of the bread under a broiler.

Cut the meatballs in half, place on the bread, and cover with ¼ C grated cheese.

Return to the broiler to melt the cheese.

Ladle ¼ C sauce onto the meatballs.

Use leftover meatloaf or grilled
sausage in place of meatballs.

BEANS

4

In our house a pot of beans is a meal unto itself. Beans served on brown rice or cornbread garnished with cilantro, cheese, chopped jalapeños peppers, cubed avocado, and freshly squeezed lime juice is more than satisfying.

In New Orleans there is a tradition of red beans and rice as the standard Monday meal. Historically, Monday was washday. There was not enough time to do the laundry by hand and cook dinner. So, you put on a pot of red beans. To this day, people eat red beans on Mondays.

All the bean recipes are similar—dried beans, a seasoning meat, beer or wine, and spices. Cooking time varies according to the type of beans.

Generally speaking, I like to season my beans with lean meats and sausages like ham, ham hocks, or Andouille sausage. I suggest using whatever you find locally. If you want to make a vegetarian batch, try using hot or mild smoked paprika as a seasoning.

If you are short on time, use a 1-lb. bag of frozen seasoning blend that contains onions, peppers, and celery.

Put your beans on and go about your chores. At the end of the day, dinner will be ready.

BLACK BEANS AND RICE

(serves 8)

2 lb. black beans, rinsed
2 C onions, chopped
1 C celery, chopped
1 C red bell pepper, chopped
6 cloves garlic, chopped
2 C red wine
1 lb. spicy sausage, sliced in ¼" pieces
1 tbsp. chili powder
1 tbsp. cumin powder
1tbsp. salt
1 tsp. black pepper
3 qt. of water
4 C cooked rice (see Building Blocks)
½ C each green onions, cilantro, and jalapeño pepper, chopped
1 avocado, cubed
2 limes, cut into wedges
1 C grated queso fresco or cheese of your choice

Put the beans, onions, celery, red bell pepper, garlic, wine, sausage, chili powder, cumin, salt, pepper, and water into a large stockpot.

Bring to a boil.

Reduce heat, cover, and simmer 4 to 5 hours, stirring occasionally.

If the beans have too much liquid, simmer uncovered once the beans are soft.

Serve the beans and rice.

Have the green onions, cilantro, pepper, avocado, limes, and cheese on the table to be used as condiments.

Try serving the black beans on tortilla chips.

Make a meal of black beans and rice with Debris and a salad.

For vegetarian black beans, add 2 tbsp. smoked paprika and 2 tbsp. olive oil.

RED BEANS AND RICE
(serves 8)

2 lb. red beans, rinsed
2 C onions, chopped
1 C celery, chopped
1 C red bell pepper, chopped
6 cloves garlic, chopped
1 lb. sausage, cut into ¼" pieces
½ lb. ham, chopped
2 bay leaves
1 tbsp. each thyme, oregano,
   basil, black pepper, salt, and
   Tabasco sauce
2 C red wine or beer
3 qt. water
4 C cooked rice (see Building
Blocks)

Put all the ingredients in a stock-pot, except for the cooked rice.

Bring to a boil.

Reduce heat, cover, and simmer for 2-3 hours, stirring occasionally.

If the beans have too much liquid, simmer uncovered once the beans are soft.

Season with salt, pepper, and Tabasco sauce to taste.

Remove the bay leaves before serving.

TIDBITS

If you don't have time to chop the vegetables, use a bag of frozen seasoning blend.

The amount of salt may need adjustment depending on what type of sausage or ham used.

One of my favorite types of meat to use is tasso, a very lean, heavily smoked piece of pork. You may be able to find it in the grocery store.

For vegetarian beans, add 2 tbsp. smoked paprika and 2 tbsp. olive oil.

WHITE BEANS AND CORN CAKE

(serves 8)

2 lb. white beans, rinsed
2 C onions, chopped
1 C celery, chopped
1 C red bell pepper, chopped
6 cloves garlic, chopped
2 C ham, chopped
1 tbsp. salt
1 tsp. black pepper
1 tbsp. thyme
3 qt. of water
1 bottle of dark beer like a Guinness or Black Mocha Stout
Corn Cake (see Building Blocks)

Place the beans, onions, celery, bell pepper, garlic, ham, salt, pepper, thyme, beer, and water in a large stockpot.

Bring to a boil.

Reduce heat, cover, and simmer 4-5 hours, stirring occasionally.

If the beans have too much liquid, simmer uncovered once the beans are soft.

Correct the salt and pepper to taste.

Bake the Corn Cake.

To serve, place piece of cornbread in the bottom of a bowl and ladle a cup of beans on top.

If you don't have time to make the Corn Cake, pick some up at the grocery store bakery or use a mix.

For vegetarian beans, add 2 tbsp. smoked paprika and 2 tbsp. olive oil.

5

SOUPS

Soups are a healthy and hearty meal any time of year. Mexicans believe a hot and spicy soup in warm weather will actually cool you down.

My favorite soup is Rejuvenation soup. There is something so nourishing about the combination of greens, butternut squash, and fennel seeds. When a friend of mine had surgery, she asked me to fill her freezer with Rejuvenation soup so she could eat it every day during her recovery. My friend told her doctor that she believed her recovery was so quick as a result of the soup.

Soups are best when started with homemade stock. If time is an issue, do not hesitate to use organic low salt stocks available in grocery stores.

Fresh vegetables are best but I have no problem using frozen vegetables like okra or butternut squash. I am not beyond using frozen bags of chopped onions, peppers, and celery. Vegetables can be roasted before adding to the pot for a deeper flavor.

A bowl of soup and a piece of crusty fresh bread is a wonderful thing.

CHICKEN AND SAUSAGE GUMBO

(serves 8)

1 C canola oil
1 C white flour
2 onions, chopped
1 red bell pepper, chopped
3 stalks celery, chopped
6 cloves garlic, chopped
1 tbsp. thyme
1 tsp. oregano
1 tsp. basil
½ tsp. cayenne pepper
1 tsp. salt
2 bay leaves
1 tbsp. Tabasco sauce
1 lb. Andouille sausage or cooked local sausage, cut lengthwise
　and sliced
1 roasted chicken, picked into bite size pieces
1-2 qt. chicken stock (see Building Blocks)
2 lb. frozen sliced okra
3 tbsp. parsley, chopped
3 tbsp. green onions, chopped
4 C cooked rice (see Building Blocks)

TIDBITS

The gumbo is best when made at least a day before serving.

If you have never made a roux, you might want to look up a video on YouTube.

Be sure to freeze a couple of quarts before serving because it will disappear.

This is a very easy recipe to double—more for the freezer.

In a large cast iron pot, heat the oil on medium heat.

When it is hot, add the flour using a whisk to stir into the oil.

Reduce the heat to low and continuously whisk, being sure to thoroughly scrape the bottom of the pot.

The flour will slowly begin to change from white to light brown to a chocolate brown.

As soon as the roux is a chocolate brown, quickly add all the vegetables and stir.

Add 1 C of chicken stock and mix well.

Simmer this mixture for 20 minutes.

Add the sausage, okra, remainder of the chicken stock, thyme, oregano, basil, cayenne pepper, bay leaves, and Tabasco sauce.

Simmer for 1 hour, covered.

It should have the consistency of a thick soup. Add more stock if it is too thick, or simmer with the lid off to thicken.

Before serving, remove the bay leaves and add the parsley and green onions.

Serve over rice.

GUMBO Z'HERBES

(serves 8)

1 C canola oil
1 C white flour
2 onions, chopped
1 red bell pepper, chopped
3 stalks celery, chopped
6 cloves garlic chopped
1 tbsp. thyme
1 tsp. oregano
1 tsp. basil
½ tsp. cayenne pepper
1 tsp. salt
2 bay leaves
2 tbsp. smoked paprika
1 tbsp. Tabasco sauce
1-2 qt. vegetable stock (see Building Blocks)
2 lb. frozen sliced okra
2 C cabbage, sliced
2 C collards, sliced
2 C turnip greens, sliced
2 C Swiss chard, sliced
3 tbsp. parsley, chopped
3 tbsp. green onions, chopped
4 C cooked rice (see Building Blocks)

In a large cast iron pot, heat the oil on medium heat.

When it is hot, add the flour using a whisk to stir into the oil.

Reduce the heat to low and continuously whisk, being sure to thoroughly scrape the bottom of the pot.

The flour will slowly begin to change from white to light brown to a chocolate brown.

As soon as the roux is a chocolate brown, quickly add all the vegetables and stir.

TIDBITS

The gumbo is best when made at least a day before serving.

If you have never made a roux, you might want to look up a video on YouTube.

Be sure to freeze a couple of quarts before serving because it will disappear.

This is a very easy recipe to double—more for the freezer.

Add 1 C of vegetable stock and mix well.

Simmer this mixture for 20 minutes.

Add the okra, all of the greens, remainder of the vegetable stock, thyme, oregano, basil, cayenne pepper, bay leaves, and Tabasco sauce.

Simmer for 1 hour, covered.

It should have the consistency of a thick soup. Add more stock if it is too thick, or simmer with the lid off to thicken.

Before serving, remove the bay leaves and add the parsley and green onions.

Serve over rice.

LEMON VEGETABLE SOUP

(serves 8)

3 qt. chicken or vegetable stock (see Building Blocks)
2 15-oz. cans of chopped tomatoes
2 tbsp. olive oil
2 onions, chopped
3 stalks celery, chopped
3 carrots, sliced
6 garlic cloves, sliced
2 medium eggplants, peeled, sliced, and cubed
2 zucchini, cut lengthwise and sliced
2 yellow squash, cut lengthwise and sliced
1 lb. fresh spinach
1 tbsp. thyme
1 tsp. oregano
1 tsp. basil
1 tbsp. salt
1 tsp. pepper
3 tbsp. lemon juice
Zest of 1 lemon
1 C crumbled feta cheese
2 C orzo pasta, cooked according to directions

TIDBITS

Add the meat of a roasted chicken if you want a heartier soup.

Garnish with fresh mint leaves, if available.

Garnish with crushed pita chips.

Add any other vegetables you might have on hand.

I try to keep this soup in the freezer. It is so refreshing to have when returning from travelling.

In a large stockpot, sauté onions, celery, carrots, and garlic in the olive oil for 10 minutes.

Add stock, tomatoes, eggplant, thyme, oregano, basil, salt, and pepper.

Simmer for 1 hour, covered.

Add zucchini and yellow squash.

Simmer for 20 minutes.

Add the spinach, lemon juice, and lemon zest.

Simmer for 5 minutes.

To serve, place ½ C of orzo in a bowl, ladle 1 C of soup over it, and garnish with feta cheese.

MEXICAN CHICKEN SOUP

(serves 8)

3 qt. chicken stock (see Building Blocks)
5 dried ancho chilies
2 tbsp. olive oil
3 onions, chopped
2 red bell peppers, chopped
6 garlic cloves, chopped
2 jars green salsa
2 roasted chickens, picked into bite size pieces
1 tbsp. salt
2 tbsp. cumin powder
1 tbsp. Tabasco sauce
½ C each cilantro, green onions, chopped jalapeño pepper, and
   chopped avocado
1 C grated queso fresco
2 limes, cut into wedges
2 C cooked rice (see Building Blocks) or 4 C tortilla chips

Simmer the chicken stock and dried chilies for 1 hour.
The broth should turn dark.

Strain the stock to remove the peppers and seeds.

Sauté the onions, peppers, and garlic in olive oil until lightly brown.

Add the chicken stock, salsa, salt,
cumin powder, and Tabasco sauce.

Simmer for 1 hour.

Add the chicken.

Simmer for 15 minutes.

Correct seasoning to taste.

Serve over rice or tortilla chips.

Garnish with cilantro, green onions, jalapeño peppers, avocados,
cheese, and lime.

Substitute 2 tbsp. ancho
chili powder for the
ancho chilies.

REJUVENATION SOUP
(Serves 8)

3 qt. chicken stock (see Building Blocks)
3 tbsp. olive oil
2 large onions, chopped
5 cloves garlic, chopped
4 tbsp. fennel seeds
2 large butternut squash, peeled, and cubed
2 15-oz. cans white beans, rinsed and drained
1 lb. greens such as chard, spinach, kale, or collards, chopped
2 roasted chickens, picked into bite size pieces
1 tbsp. salt
1 tbsp. pepper

TIDBITS

Use your largest stockpot to accommodate the greens.

Frozen greens and squash can be used as a short cut.

In place of or in addition to the chicken, add 1 lb. of Italian sausage that has been removed from the casing and browned in a skillet.

It can become a vegetarian soup by eliminating the chicken and using vegetable stock in place of the chicken stock.

Add leftover roasted vegetables.

Age enhances the flavor so it is best made a day ahead.

Be sure to put 2 containers in the freezer for another day.

Put the butternut squash in a 2" deep casserole dish and drizzle with olive oil. Place in the oven at 450 degrees for 15 minutes. Toss, then for bake for 15 minutes more. Remove from oven.

While the squash is roasting, brown the onions and garlic in olive oil in a large stockpot.

When the onions are caramelized (deeply browned), add the fennel seeds, salt, and pepper.

Sauté for 2 minutes.

Add the chicken stock, beans, and squash.

Simmer, covered, for 30 minutes.

Add the chicken.

Simmer, covered, for 20 minutes.

If using tougher greens like kale or collards, add now.

If using tender greens like spinach or chard, add at the end of the cooking time and allow to sit for 5 minutes.

Add salt and pepper to taste.

TURKEY SOUP
(serves 8)

3 qt. turkey stock or chicken stock (see Building Blocks)
3 onions, chopped
3 stalks celery, chopped
3 carrots, sliced
6 cloves garlic, chopped
4 C turkey meat, picked from the carcass into bite size pieces
1 2-lb. bag frozen sliced okra
1 tbsp. salt
1 tbsp. thyme
2 bay leaves
1 tsp. black pepper
4 C cooked rice (see Building Blocks)

TIDBITS

I make this soup as the final meal the day after Thanksgiving and declare the cooking frenzy over. This light simple soup seems to agree with everyone after a day of indulgence.

I don't believe that you can only roast a turkey during the holidays. It is a great meal anytime of year. Try roasting a turkey in March. Use as a main meal, make sandwiches, reserve some of the meat for soup (freezes well), and make a stock. For a family of four, you can create 6 different meals from one turkey. Economical and nutritious.

If you don't have turkey, substitute chicken.

Put all the ingredients except the turkey meat and okra into the stockpot.

Simmer, covered, for 2 hours, stirring occasionally.

Add the okra and the turkey meat.

Simmer, covered, for ½ hour.

Correct the seasoning to your taste.

Serve over rice.

6

LAGNIAPPE/EXTRAS

L agniappe is a French word used in southern
Louisiana to mean a little something extra, as in a
baker's dozen. These "extra" recipes do not fit into the
previous categories. People have requested them over
the years. Some are quick and easy, like the Southwestern Chicken Casserole; others, such as the Chicken
Curry, take more time, but are well worth the effort.

The Chicken Curry is a dish my mother served for
dinner parties. It is a very festive dish; the house smells
wonderful; guests are curious and excited about the
condiments. It makes for a lively meal.

CABBAGE AND RED BEAN COLESLAW

(serves 8)

3 C finely shredded cabbage
½ C red bell pepper, chopped
½ C green onions, chopped
½ C parsley, finely chopped
1 15-oz. can kidney beans, rinsed and drained
½ C feta cheese, crumbled
3 tbsp. lemon juice
3 tbsp. olive oil
Salt and pepper to taste

Combine the cabbage, bell pepper, green onions, parsley, kidney beans, and cheese.

Drizzle with lemon juice and olive oil.

Toss.

Add salt and pepper to taste.

TIDBITS

This is a great vegetarian dish to take to a potluck.

Leftovers make a great lunch.

Keeps well in the refrigerator for a couple of days.

For convenience, I purchase a 10-oz. bag of angel hair cabbage from the produce section.

CHICKEN CURRY

(serves 4)

½ C canola oil
½ C flour
2 onions, chopped
2 stalks celery, chopped
6 cloves garlic, chopped
2 Granny Smith apples, peeled, cored, and chopped
3 tbsp. yellow curry powder
1 tsp. salt
1 qt. chicken stock (see Building Blocks)
1 roasted chicken, picked into bite size pieces
½ C each peanuts, coconut flakes, currants, and chopped
    hard boiled egg
5 strips bacon, cooked and crumbled
1 C yogurt
Chutney
2 C rice cooked (see Building Blocks)

TIDBITS

It is best made a day ahead of time so the flavors can mingle.

Adjust the consistency with more stock if it is too thick or simmer uncovered if it is too thin. It should not be soupy.

This recipe can be vegetarian by replacing the chicken with vegetables. Cauliflower and eggplant are delicious with curry.

As always, it freezes beautifully. A nice thing to have stashed away for a cold winter's meal.

In a large cast iron pot, heat the oil on a medium heat.

When the oil is hot, whisk in the flour.

Continue whisking for 2-3 minutes. The mixture will turn a light beige.

Add all the vegetables, curry powder, and stock. Stir.

Cover and simmer for 1 hour, stirring occasionally so it doesn't stick to the bottom of the pot.

Add the chicken.

Correct the seasoning. Add more curry powder if you want a stronger flavor.

Put small bowls of all the condiments on the table.

To serve, place ½ C rice in a bowl and ladle 1 C curry on top.

MEDITERRANEAN RICE

serves 4

4 C cooked brown rice (see Building Blocks)
16 oz. steamed or canned lentils, rinsed and drained
6 onions, thinly sliced
½ C olive oil
1 tbsp. cumin powder
1 tsp. cinnamon
1 tsp. salt
½ tsp. red pepper flakes

While the rice is cooking, heat the oil in a large cast iron pot.

Add the onions.

Over a medium heat cook the onions until they caramelize (deep brown). Stir frequently.

The onions will shrink down considerably. It could take ½ hour.

When the onions are brown, add the cumin powder, cinnamon, salt, and red pepper flakes.

Add the rice and mix well.

Correct the seasoning to your taste.

TIDBITS

This recipe can be made with leftover rice.

I buy packaged steamed lentils from the produce section.

The rice is a nice accompaniment to grilled chicken or steak. Add a pan of roasted vegetables and you have a nice meal.

Leftovers are great for lunch with some yogurt and left-over chutney.

This is one of the few dishes I do not freeze. Rice just doesn't do well when frozen.

ROASTED VEGETABLES

Vegetables
Olive oil
1 tsp. salt
1 tsp. pepper
Additional seasonings such as thyme, basil, oregano,
    herbs de Provence, and balsamic vinegar

Heat the oven to 450 degrees.

Cut up the vegetables and place in a casserole dish with 2" sides.

Drizzle with olive oil. Add seasoning. Toss.

Place in the oven for 15 minutes.

Toss and roast for another 15 minutes.

Vegetables should be slightly browned.

Choose vegetables with similar cooking times to roast
together. For example squash, eggplant, asparagus, and
broccoli (which are water based) require less time than
root vegetables.

Roast red beets by themselves or they will bleed into the
other vegetables—not very attractive.

SUGGESTED COMBINATIONS

Potatoes, cut in lengthwise spears or baby new potatoes cut in half. Add a seasoned salt.

Purple potatoes, cut in half, and sweet potatoes, cut in spears. Add a seasoned salt and herbs.

Brussel sprouts, cut in half, a chopped onion. Add salt, pepper, and 2 tbsp. of balsamic vinegar.

Orange beets, peeled, daikon radish, and turnips, sliced. Add seasoned salt.

Asparagus with salt, pepper, and a squeeze of lemon juice. Roast for only 10 minutes.

Eggplant, sliced. Add thyme, oregano, basil, salt, and pepper.

Zucchini, yellow squash, onion, sliced. Add herbs de Provence.

Leeks, parsnips and carrots, sliced. Add a seasoned salt.

SMOKED PAPRIKA SALAD DRESSING

2 tsp. smoked paprika
2 tsp. salt
1 tsp. sugar
1 tsp. coarse ground mustard
¼ tsp. Cayenne pepper
1 C apple cider vinegar or rice vinegar
½ C olive oil
¼ C water
4 fat garlic cloves, peeled

Mix all ingredients in a container with a lid. Adjust the amount of vinegar to suit the level of acidity you like by adding water or olive oil.

The salad dressing has a distinctly different flavor with the smoked paprika. It elevates the simplest of salads.

SOUTHWESTERN CHICKEN CASSEROLE

(Serves 8)

1 48-oz. jar salsa
1 15-oz. can black beans, rinsed and drained
1 15-oz. can corn, drained
2 tbsp. cumin powder
1 tbsp. chili powder
1 roasted chicken, picked and in bite size pieces
1 13-oz. bag tortilla chips, crushed
2 C water or chicken stock
2 limes, juiced
3 C queso fresco or cheese of your choice
½ C each green onions, cilantro, and jalapeño peppers, finely
   chopped
1 lime, cut into wedges
1 C sour cream

Preheat the oven to 350 degrees.

In a large Dutch oven heat the salsa over a medium heat for
5 minutes.

Add the black beans, corn, chicken, lime juice, and mix.

Add the crushed tortilla chips and mix.

Add water or chicken stock.

The mixture should be the consistency of mush.

Stir in 2 C of cheese.

Heat thoroughly.

Adjust seasoning to taste. Usually no need for extra salt.

Put the mixture in a 9 x 13" casserole dish.

Cover with foil and bake for 30 minutes.

Serve with the green onions, jalapeños, cilantro, lime, sour cream, and extra cheese as condiments.

TIDBITS

If you are making the dish to eat immediately, skip the casserole and just serve it out of the pot.

It is a great dish to make on a night that all the family is arriving for a holiday. It can sit on the stove until each person is ready to eat.

This dish has been well received at beach trips by family members young and old—a universal dish.

CPSIA information can be obtained at www.ICGtesting.com
Printed in the USA
BVOW11s0604201015

423191BV00007B/8/P